i

PEPPERBACK PRESS

The *Sighthound* ADOPTION HANDBOOK

by

Michael Owens

Contents

Preface

This handbook has lived for over ten years in various forms, and it was inspired by similar documents that existed for years before that. Every reputable adoption group sends their dogs (or cats or guinea pigs or parrots, etc.) home with documentation. The first part of that documentation is specific to the animal. It often includes their vaccine history, medical records, and other important information specific to that pet. The other part of that documentation varies greatly from organization to organization.

It is common for Greyhound groups to provide particularly robust information to their adopters. There are two articles that most groups send home with their Greyhounds, and you will see them included in this handbook. The article by Sharon Mathers entitled "Trust — A Deadly Disease" is a staple of the adoption community. While it was written with Greyhounds in mind, it is applicable to all dogs and should be required reading for every adopter.

The other required reading is "What's in those Blood Tests?" by Suzanne Stack, DVM. This article was also written for Greyhound adopters, but the information it contains is applicable to most sighthound breeds as well. It is important for both adopters and their veterinarians to have these values on hand and refer to them whenever analyzing test results.

In addition to these well-known resources, this handbook also includes the knowledge of hundreds of volunteers—collected and distilled over the course of many years. We send it out into the world in the hopes that it will benefit sighthounds and their owners.

Michael Owens, Director
The Sighthound Underground

Introduction

The Sighthound Underground was born from the decline of the Greyhound racing industry in the United States. Many of the original adopters, foster parents, and volunteers who made SHUG possible, had experience as volunteers for groups that place retired racing Greyhounds. There they had an excellent vantage point from which to observe the decline of the adoptable Greyhound population. Every year there were fewer and fewer dogs available.

When SHUG was founded, the goal of the volunteers was to repurpose the existing networks and strategies that had supported Greyhound adoption for decades, to help other sighthounds in need.

Once a potential adopter complained about our group's terrible "customer service". On another occasion a man likened the experience of adopting a dog to buying a car.

We explained to both gentlemen, very firmly, that they were sadly mistaken. Neither of these men were our customers.

When you adopt, you are not buying and we are not selling.

We are serving, and it is not the humans that are our clients.

In our version of The Bachelor, potential mates are carefully vetted. While the gentlemen above were waiting to be flattered and courted, our team of volunteers were busy judging them. We are not unkind, but we are thorough. The matches we make have to survive not just a night—or a season—but a lifetime.

In one way or another, all of the dogs we place are special needs.

They are old or broken or old *and* broken. They are not a commodity or even an asset. They are a dependent and a liability. They are a child who will never move out and get a job. When you adopt a dog you are signing a contract to feed them, provide vet care, and pay to replace the remotes they eat. You are taking on the obligation to sooth the asses they bite. And yes, all of this can be a terrible responsibility.

Occasionally we will receive an application from someone who wants an emotional support dog or service dog. Again, we explain to them that is not what we do. We are not here to support you. We are here to support them.

The relationships that we make when we match dogs to humans are not balanced and that is by design. We are not looking for an adopter to love a dog as much as they will love them in return. We want adopters who would love our dogs ten times—a hundred times—more.

Our dogs need someone who will love them when they are pouting because breakfast is ten minutes late. They need someone who will love them when they are stressed out during thunderstorms and poop on their floor.

Our dogs need **Emotional Support Humans**.

So before you apply to adopt, ask yourself if you can be there for a dog? When they are old and cranky? When they are scared and bark at the mailman? When they get confused and eat your favorite shoes?

To be very, very clear, you are not buying a shirt or a car. You are applying for a job. This job has no salary, no 401K, no healthcare. This job is first, second, AND third shift. This job has no growth potential and will almost certainly end in tears. It does, however, have fantastic fringe benefits.

This is not your dog. But if you are very, very lucky, you might be their human.

Community and Communication

People ask us all the time if adoption fees are tax deductible. For that you have to ask an accountant. What we can tell you is that the dog you have adopted is not an asset. You didn't get something for your adoption fee that will ever make you rich. You've signed a contract that you won't race them for money, sell them for profit, or breed them.

What you have taken on is—in all practical terms—a liability. You've signed a contract that you will pay for your dog's vet care, monthly heartworm and flea/tick prevention, nutritious food, and whatever vaccinations and registrations your area requires. You have to keep them in collars (it isn't spelled out in the contract but let's face it, dogs this pretty need some fancy damn collars) and you've taken on the responsibility for whatever they destroy or eat.

When you adopt a dog you are taking on a burden. Not just to provide for them financially, but also their physical and emotional needs as well.

Before you become too discouraged, there is some good news. Along with that dog comes a network. This network stretches from coast to coast in North America and around the world. There are sighthound people in every corner of the planet and they are ready to support you.

You'll find a chapter in this book about lost dogs. Not to scare you, but to prepare you and drive home the message that communication is key. You are not in this alone. Your dog has a backup plan. Their backup plan has a backup plan.

Wherever you are—at this moment and in the future—there will be sighthound people. Find them. Whether you need someone to watch your pup for a weekend or talk you down from the ledge after hearing the "Scream of Death" for the first time, being a member of multiple sighthound groups will improve you and your dog's quality of life.

The first place to start is with your adoption group. If you adopted from Sighthound Underground, we have public pages on most social media platforms as well as a private group on Facebook that is very active. Ask your application processor or adoption coordinator if you haven't received your invitation to the group. There are over 500 members located all over the world. Someone is awake. No matter what time it is, ask your question and someone will be there with an answer or advice.

The SHUG Facebook group is also a "No Judgement Zone". The group is private so that members can ask questions or share stories they aren't comfortable posting on their public pages.

We talk about poop. A lot.

There are other Greyhound, sighthound, and general dog groups in every state, every town. Find your tribe. Because no matter how careful you are, the day will come when you will need their support.

Sighthounds 101

What are sighthounds? In North America the most common sighthound is the **Greyhound**, but a sighthound is—literally—a dog that hunts by sight (as opposed to scent). You can usually pick sighthounds out of a crowd due to their very distinctive anatomy. Tall and thin, even the smaller breeds of sighthound will have the deep chests and high tucks that define these special dogs. In addition, there is a correlation between muzzle length and visual acuity, so sighthounds are known for their long, sleek muzzles.

Their unique physique doesn't stop there, however. As dogs bred to hunt, sighthounds are some of the fastest animals on land, and it shows. Like human runners, sighthounds are long and lean. The Greyhounds commonly found in North America are English racing Greyhounds, which were bred to sprint. Consequently, they have large, round thigh muscles that are super satisfying to slap.

The Greyhound's Spanish cousin, the **Galgo**, were bred to hunt wild hare across the vast plains of Spain. They are more marathon runners than sprinters and their thigh muscles tend to be flatter. In general, Galgos are slightly smaller than greyhounds, have longer tails, more decorative ears, and come in a wirehair coat as well as the more familiar smooth coat.

Comparisons between Greyhounds and Galgos are common, but their similarities vastly outweigh their differences. The primary distinction between the two is in their upbringing. Racing Greyhounds are traditionally raised in a structured kennel environment. They are used to being crated, especially at night. Galgos, however, often come into rescue as strays. Even with their owners, they are commonly let off lead to hunt and used to much more freedom. Although both Greyhounds and Galgos typically come to adoption groups having never lived in a traditional home environment, they both adapt well to the pampered pet lifestyle.

From the frozen north of the Russian Empire, the **Borzoi** have been called the "cold weather" version of the Greyhound. In addition to their larger builds, Borzoi (or Russian Wolfhounds) have much heavier coats. Like Greyhounds and Galgos, Borzoi come in a vast array of coat colors. They also have a range of coat textures from silky and flat to various degrees of dense and curly. A Borzoi may be as low maintenance as a Flat-Coated Retriever or shed as much as a Siberian Husky.

The fleet-footed **Saluki** is bred to run through the desert. Like most sighthounds they love nothing more than to roast themselves on a hot patio—making you take on the role of mean mom (or dad) to get them out of the sun. Like the Galgo, Salukis come in two coats. The smooth Saluki is often mistake for a Greyhound or Galgo. The feathered Saluki is more common in the United States, with the distinctive "feathers" on ears and tails. As with Borzoi, the feathered Saluki coat can vary and some pups may have minimal feathering while some may have considerable hair that is long and thick.

When it comes to coat, the **Afghan Hound** takes the prize. That beauty does come with a price, though, and they are also the most high maintenance of all of the sighthound breeds. Luckily, most Afghans are quite comfortable with being groomed—and expect their human servants to cater to their needs on a daily basis.

Anecdotally, when it comes to personality, Saluki and Afghan Hound females can be among the most high maintenance of dogs. They have high expectations and can be quite vocal if their owners don't meet them. In addition to singing the song of their people, these divas have been known to dish out discipline with the slap of a paw as well.

While many people describe **Whippets** as pocket Greyhounds, they are a very different dog when it comes to personality. Generally speaking, Greyhounds and the other larger sighthound breeds are the fastest couch potatoes on the planet. A Greyhound may be able to achieve speeds of up to 45mph in three steps...but the fourth step is back towards the couch they came off of. Whippets, on the other hand, are a much "sportier" dog and tend to enjoy being on the go.

Likewise, **Ibizan Hounds** and the other Spanish breeds that are known colloquially as **Podencos**, tend to be more active and well-suited to canine sports. From the red Andalusian Hounds to the large wirehair Companeros to the Dachshund-shaped Manetos, Pods are the Jack Russels of the sighthound world. They are up for anything and the perfect companion for avid out-doors-people.

At the other end of the sighthound spectrum, the tiny **Italian Greyhound** has no functional purpose beyond stealing their owner's body heat and taking the fashion world by storm. Don't tell them, though. Especially as puppies, they are completely unaware of their own fragility. Sadly, we have seen many Italian

Greyhounds with broken legs from nothing more strenuous than jumping off of the couch.

There are more breeds of sighthounds around the world, including the majestic Scottish Deerhounds and Irish Wolfhounds. From the regal Azawakh from western Africa to the Rajapalayam from southern India, sighthounds share a commonality beyond their anatomy. Sighthounds were bred—for thousands of years—to work with humans. We belong together.

Your New Dog

Congratulations! If you've made it through the application process and adopted a sighthound, you have joined a ~~cult~~ special group of people. Now what? Well, here are some tips and tricks to start your new family member off on the right path. Take some time these first few days to get on the right path and the next fifteen years will be a lot easier!

Who's your daddy?

If you adopted a dog from the Sighthound Underground, they will come home with two collars. The smaller collar is a **tag collar** (in basic black it goes with everything—so LEAVE IT ON!) with a SHUG ID tag, but you should also add your own tag with your info to it as well. If your dog came from another group, you can pick up a thin, lightweight, buckle or snap collar at any pet store to use as a tag collar. We love the flat style tags that slip or clip onto the collar and don't jingle.

The larger collar your sighthound wears is called a **martingale**. Martingale collars are designed to tighten when the leash is pulled. Unlike choke collars, a martingale is a "limited" slip collar, which means it will not tighten enough to hurt your

11

dog, just enough to keep the collar from going over their small, wedge-shaped head. Most martingales do not have a buckle or snap. Instead you loosen them every time you take them off and then tighten them when you put them back on. Tightening your dog's martingale collar every time you attach the leash to it is a good habit to get into. You should **not** be able to pull it over their head when it is fitted properly.

While we're talking about tags and identification, if you're changing your dog's name (and even if you aren't) don't forget to play the **Name Game**! Grab a handful of treats or kibble while you're watching your favorite show. Every now and then, call your dog's name in a happy voice. When they look at you, toss them a treat. It's a great start to building a solid working relationship and begin bonding.

The Drag Queen

No, not that kind of drag! (Although we promise not to judge you if you paint his nails.) But what we really want to see dragging is the leash! For the first three days, keep your dog on leash inside and out. When they're outside--even in a fenced yard--hold onto the leash with the super-duper **Slip Knot**. Don't know what that is? Don't worry, we'll explain in a future chapter.

When you're inside, just let your dog drag the leash. This makes it easy to grab them when needed--especially if they're a little shy. You can just step on the leash as they go by and not have to grab at their collar. But even more importantly, it makes you much more aware of their movements, which is a big help with house training.

When your new dog leaves the room, chances are they're looking for a place to potty. As you catch the tail end of the leash as it rounds the corner, just walk them right outside. Remember to throw a party with lots of happy voice when they produce outside. If your neighbors aren't worried about your mental health, you aren't doing it right.

Height Requirement

Your new dog isn't a rollercoaster—but there is a height requirement to take him for a spin. We know the kids want to help, but this isn't the time. Even the big kids need to wait a while. For these first three days at least, your dog should only go out for a **walk** with mom or dad.

Especially if you don't have any other pets, you need to learn the squirrel traps in the neighborhood and which yards harbor attractive nuisances on your daily walk route. Once you've identified and clearly marked the fluffies, nutties, and barkers in your environment, walks will be a little more manageable.

The Natives are Restless

The native pets, that is. Take the time making **introductions** to your resident pets. We LOVE the hard plastic **basket muzzles** that racing Greyhounds wear and we'll talk more about those later. Always make sure small dogs and cats have an escape path.

If possible, the first time butt-sniffing is best done outside. Depending on just how many dogs you have in your pack, do introductions in small groups to avoid overwhelming the new guy. Keep basket muzzles on when you move everyone inside, and monitor group dynamics over the next few days.

Are tails wagging? Ears relaxed? Encourage bonding with the pack by doing activities together so that your new pup will start to bond and feel like part of the household.

The House Rules

Let your dog check out the house, room by room, allowing for the requisite sniffing. Watch carefully for potential pee stops and correct immediately. At first, you might keep your new pup leashed and **tethered** to you. Tethering is fabulous for speedy bonding! When you're not around, avoid returning to find surprises by keeping them confined using an ex-pen, crate, or baby gate. Let your dog EARN access to each part of the house.

The Great Outdoors

Unfamiliar sights and sounds can give anybody a jolt, so be on alert when on new adventures. Keep the walks short at first, and bring another calm dog along, if possible, for moral support.

If your new dog's level of uncertainty calls for extra care, consider using a martingale in conjunction with a **harness**. You may think you're committing a fashion faux pas, but the dog won't think less of you. Also, a **carabineer** can be double insurance that a leash clip won't give way should a dog lunge after a squirrel. And always make a **slip knot** with the leash around your wrist.

The Off Switch

When the going gets tough, the tough take a nap. If your dog is stressed or is making you stressed, you may both need a break.

These are the times when crates come in to save the day. Even a ten to fifteen minute break in their **crate** with a peanut butter filled toy like a kong can be enough to help your dog calm down and feel more secure.

When break time is over, just open the door and walk away. Don't drag them out, let them come when they're ready. If you're using a collapsible wire crate, please use **zip ties** to reinforce the connections between the front and rear panels and the sides. This will make sure that the crate can't collapse in on the dog accidentally. And remember, if they're going to be unsupervised in the crate, remove the martingale (which can get caught) but leave on their tag collar.

In all this strictness with leashes and collars, don't forget to give that new dog all the loving it needs!

The First Vet Visit

Within two weeks of adoption, you should take your dog to the vet for an introductory visit. It's a chance for your dog to meet and get comfortable with your vet when they're *not* feeling bad or in the middle of an emergency. It's also a chance for your vet to get a "baseline" on your dog. For example, if your dog isn't feeling well, and the vet asks if he's been lethargic, knowing you have a sighthound ahead of time will avoid the "my dog normally sleeps 20 hours a day" talk.

We recommend a full blood panel at your dog's first visit, especially if they are a senior. That way you have something to compare numbers against if they begin having issues down the line.

At this first visit and every annual checkup, your vet should scan your dog's microchip and listen to their heart. In addition, your vet may also suggest testing for the following, if they haven't been done recently:

- Tick-borne diseases (TBDs)

- Heartworm

- Intestinal parasites

If your dog is from Spain or another mediterranean country, your vet should check for Leishmania at every annual check-up. Many vets in the United States and Canada are not familiar with Leish, so you may need to help steer them toward some resources.

When evaluating the results of your dog's blood test results, your vet may bring up these things about your dog's health that are actually fairly normal for Sighthounds:

- Elevated BUN, creatinine, and AST levels

- Low platelets (under 100K, run a TBD panel)

- High red blood cell count (PCV, Hct)

- Low white blood cells (WBCs)

- Low thyroid values (if there are also behavioral issues or coat changes, you may to consider supplements)

- Enlarged heart

- Heart murmur

The next chapter will address these issues in detail and it is a good idea to make a copy and bring it with you on your first vet visit. Make sure your vet includes this information in your dog's chart for future reference.

"What's in those Blood Tests?"

By Susanne Stack, DVM

Blood Tests

When your veterinarian sends your Greyhound's blood to a lab, she/he is most commonly asking the lab to run a **CBC** (Complete Blood Count). This common analysis covers these items:

- RBC = Red Blood Cells

- Hgb = Hemoglobin

- PCV / HCT = Packed Cell Volume/Hematocrit

- WBC = White Blood Cells

- Platelets = Help to form blood clots to stop bleeding.

For a more in-depth look, usually to determine kidney/liver functions, your veterinarian may also ask for a **"Chem Panel."** This will give them information about:

- T.P. = Total Protein Globulin

- Creatinine = A waste product filtered out of the blood by the kidneys.

- T4 = Thyroid level

If you don't understand what your veterinarian has ordered, ask for details!

Greyhound blood work has enough differences from "other dog" blood work to sometimes make it deceivingly "normal" or "abnormal" if your veterinarian isn't familiar with these differences. The salient differences are discussed below.

Greyhounds:
- RBC: 7.4 - 9.0

- Hgb: 19.0 - 21.5

- PCV: 55 – 65

Other Breeds:
- RBC: 5.5 - 8.5

- Hgb: 12.0 - 18.0

- PCV: 37 – 55

Never accept a diagnosis of **Polycythemia**—a once-in-a-lifetime rare diagnosis of pathologic red blood cell overproduction—in a Greyhound.

Conversely, never interpret a Greyhound PCV in the 30s-40s as being normal just because it is for other dogs. A Greyhound with a PCV in the 30s-40s is an anemic Greyhound. Generally, a Greyhound PCV less than 50 is a red flag to check for **Ehrlichia**.

WBC

- Greyhound: 3.5 - 6.5

- Other dog: 6.0 - 17.0

Other Greyhound CBC changes are less well known. The Greyhound's normally low WBC has caused more than one healthy Greyhound to undergo a bone marrow biopsy in search of cancer or some other cause of the "low WBC."

Platelets

- Greyhound: 80,000 - 200,000

- Other dog: 150,000 - 400,000

Greyhound platelet numbers are lower on average than other dog breeds, which might be mistakenly interpreted as a problem. It is thought that Greyhound WBCs, platelets, and total protein may be lower to physiologically "make room" in the bloodstream for the increased red cell load.

Compounding these normally low WBC and platelet numbers is the fact that Ehrlichia, a common blood parasite of Greyhounds, can lower WBC and platelet counts. So if there is any doubt as to whether the WBC / platelet counts are normal, an Ehrlichia titer is always in order. The other classic changes with Ehrlichia are lowered PCV and elevated total protein. But bear in mind that every Greyhound will not have every change, and Ehrlichia Greyhounds can have normal CBCs.

T.P. & Globulin

- Greyhound TP: 4.5 - 6.0

- Other dog TP: 5.4 - 7.8

- Greyhound Globulin: 2.1 - 3.2

- Other dog Globulin: 2.8 - 4.2

Greyhound total proteins tend to run on the low end of normal. T.P.s in the 5.0s and 6.0s are the norm. While the albumin fraction of T.P. is the same as other dogs, the globulin component is lower.

Creatinine

- Greyhound: 0.8 - 1.6

- Other dogs: 0.0 - 1.0

Greyhound creatinines run higher than other breeds as a function of their large lean muscle mass. A study at the Auburn University College of Veterinary Medicine found that 80% of retired racing Greyhounds they sampled had creatinine values above the standard reference range for "other dogs." As a lone finding, an "elevated creatinine" is not indicative of impending kidney failure. If the BUN and urinalysis are normal, so is the "elevated" creatinine.

T4 (Thyroid)

- Greyhound: 0.5 - 3.6 (mean 1.47 +/- 0.63)

- Other dogs: 1.52 - 3.60

These figures are from a University of Florida study of thyroid function in 221 Greyhounds -- 97 racers, 99 broods, and 25 studs -- so it included both racers and "retired." While Greyhound thyroid levels are a whole chapter unto themselves, a good rule of thumb is that Greyhound T4s run about half that of other breeds.[1]

Urinalysis

And lastly, the good news -- Greyhound urinalysis levels are the same as other dog breeds. It is normal for males to have small to moderate amounts of bilirubin in the urine.

Reprinted with the author's permission.

---

1. NOTE: At Sighthound Underground we encourage owners of sighthounds with clinical signs of low thyroid to try a two week course of a very low dose of thyroid supplementation. Signs of low thyroid can include increased irritability, lethargy, and hair loss or "dullness" of the coat.

Sources:

M.R. Herron, DVM, ACVS, "Clinical Pathology of the Racing Greyhound", 1991.

C. Guillermo Couto, DVM, ACVIM, "Managing Thrombocytopenia in Dogs & Cats", Veterinary Medicine, May 1999.

J.Steiss, DVM, W. Brewer, DVM, E.Welles, DVM, J. Wright, DVM, "Hematologic & Serum Biochemical Reference Values in Retired Greyhounds", Compendium on Con_ tinuing Education, March 2000.

M. Bloomberg, DVM, MS, "Thyroid Function of the Racing Greyhound", University of Florida, 1987.

D. Bruyette, DVM, ACVIM, Veterinary Information Network, 2001.

Lyme and Leish

Over the last couple of decades, ticks have become much more prevalent throughout North America and as a result, Lyme and other tick-borne diseases are endemic in many more regions. Even experienced adopters may not realize the importance of year-round flea and tick prevention in most parts of the United States.

The risks associated with Heartworm, Anaplasmosis, Babesiosis, and other less common diseases spread by these pests can be greatly reduced by the monthly application of preventives. Available as pills, topical liquids, and injections, flea and tick preventatives should be a part of your dog's regular routine.

Leishmaniasis (Leishmania or simply Leish) is a common disease in the areas around the Mediterranean Sea and is very similar to Lyme disease in the United States, which most adopters are already familiar with. Lyme can only be transmitted by ticks and Leish can only be transmitted by sand flies.

Unlike tick-borne Lyme, there is no risk of Leish to adopters. With the exception of the Gulf of Mexico, there are no tropical regions in the United States or Canada to support sand flies.

The symptoms of both diseases can be similar—and vague. They include lethargy, weight loss or loss of appetite, and general lameness or joint pain. Both diseases can cause serious kidney issues. In many cases if your vet suspects Lyme and the results are negative, a Leish test should be the next step.

in addition to the symptoms above, Leish is often accompanied by skin lesions, especially on the tips of the ears. These will be little areas that scab but never seem to heal. Nose bleeds can also be a sign of Leish (although those are more often related to dental issues).

The common treatment for Lyme is a 30 day course of doxycycline or a similar antibiotic. For Leish, the treatment depends on the severity, but miltefosine is a common option, also given as a 30 day course. Some people have a skin reaction to miltefosine, so we do recommend wearing gloves if you're administering it. Like antibiotics, it should be given with food to protect the stomach.

With both Lyme and Leish, it is important for dog parents to remember that these are not "one and done" diseases. Once your dog has been diagnosed, you need to monitor them for symptoms and do annual testing. They can flare up years later, especially in times of physical or mental stress for your dog.

The Scoop on Poop

Sighthound owners are obsessed with poop. It's a fact of life and we've grown to accept it. Since poop is one of the best indicators of health, our hyper vigilance comes in handy at times. The sad truth is that all of our sighthounds will have poop problems sooner or later. It helps to know what the poop is trying to tell you and how to deal with it effectively.

While the popular food metaphors are disgustingly amusing--who doesn't like to talk about pudding poo in front of non-dog owners?--Nestle Purina has created the definitive visual aid to help us all use the same language when it comes to discussing poop. You can find this chart in many places online.

The key to poop evaluation is moisture. There are three different ways you can judge the moisture of your dog's stool: Hardness, form, and residue. Dry poop is hard when you pick it up, separated into distinct sections (often ball-shaped), and doesn't leave any residue behind. The more moisture in your dog's poop, the softer it is to the touch and the more likely it is to be a pile (or puddle) and therefore difficult to pickup without leaving a mess.

As with most things in life, moderation in all three areas is ideal. Your dog's poop shouldn't be hard little balls but it shouldn't be a cow paddy either. Hard poop is associated with dehydration, which can be dangerous. Loose stool can be associated with a variety of problems, including intestinal parasites and inflammation caused by eating inappropriate things.

It can, however, be perfectly normal for your new arrival—permanent pack member or foster pup—to have mushy poop for the first couple of days. Normal mushy can just be part of the adjustment period. To help get things on the right track, avoid fillers and treats. Use their regular kibble while training. You can take a handful or more to dole out as rewards—just be careful to deduct that amount when mealtime rolls around.

If your dog is only eating kibble and they're still having issues, there are one of two problems. Our first guess would be intestinal parasites. Unfortunately, hookworms have become common in many Greyhound kennels over the years. Once these nasty little creatures have contaminated an area, it's nearly impossible to eradicate them.

Luckily, dewormers are generally considered extremely safe and can be given repeatedly until the issue is resolved. Ask your vet for a recommendation, but also don't be afraid to shop around for the best price. Generic versions of brand name dewormers are available and are usually much less expensive. If you're dealing with resistant hookworms, your dog may need to be on meds every two weeks for three to six months.

If your dog's fecal comes back clear, the next suspect is the kibble itself. After ten years and nearly one thousand dogs, we strongly recommend **grain-free salmon and sweet potato**-based kibble formulas. There are several brands that offer this combination at various price points.

Over recent years there have been many veterinarians voicing concern over grain-free diets and a possible link to canine dilated cardiomyopathy (DCM). These veterinarians have provided only anecdotal evidence based on a very small number of cases—literally, just a few hundred cases out of the nearly 90 million pet dogs in the United States. DCM is not common among sighthounds...but gastrointestinal issues are and they can be devastating to your dog's health and quality of life.

When switching foods, we do not recommend the traditional slow mix method. Over the years we have received many dog who we either had no idea what they were eating or no access to it (especially dogs from overseas). So rather than mix the old and new foods, when the old food is stopped abruptly, we fast the dog for 24 hours and then start the new food with a half-size portion. For the vast majority of dogs this has resulted in a much faster and easier adjustment, so it is now our preferred method.

Finally, the last thing you ever want to see in poop is a spot of red and we understand the panic it causes. But here's something to put your mind at ease: A spot or couple of drops of bright red blood, especially after a bout of diarrhea, is almost always nothing to worry about. It's the brown blood and the metallic, coppery smell in stool that necessitates a trip to the vet ASAP. The darker the stool, the more likely your dog will need veterinary care.

We hope this information helps. May your poops be firm and your poop bags strong!

Lost Dog!

We hope with all of our hearts that you will never need this information, but life happens. Be prepared. In a perfect world you are reading this in the comfort of your own home, with your dog beside you on the couch. If you're reading this because your dog is lost, here are your quick bullet points to get you through the first couple of hours.

Quick Guide

- Call out in a happy voice and say something your dog loves, like "Want to go for a RIDE?!" and run to the car and open the door. You can also try: "Who wants a treat?"; "Who's ready for dinner?"; or "Who's got the ball!"

- Grab another dog—yours or a neighbor's (unless your dog doesn't like other dogs!)—and play with the other dog, lead them into the house and see if your dog follows.

- Lie down and pretend to have a seizure. (Yes, we're totally serious.)

- CALL FOR HELP!!! If your dog has been missing for more than 10 minutes—or you don't know how long your dog has been out, it's time to ask for help. Start with your adoption group, then move onto your other dog (and non-dog) communities. Use EVERY method available for each one. For example, if you're calling SHUG, we have an 800 number, email, the Facebook page, and the private Facebook group. For your non-dog communities, don't forget your neighborhood listservs, groups, Nextdoor pages, etc. You need eyeballs!

- Make LOST DOG flyers. There is a template in this book that you can take to your local Library, UPS Store, FEDEX Kinko, or other copy shop. You can customize the flyer with your phone number and a photo of your dog if you have a clear one. We do NOT recommend using breed names, except for Greyhound. The average person isn't familiar with them. Instead, use generic terms such as "Tall Brown Dog" or "Big Fluffy Dog".

- Post LOST DOG flyers at every intersection in and out of every neighborhood. You can't put up too many flyers, but just remember that after you've found your dog they all have to come down again. If the weather is bad, use plastic sheet protectors (upside down) to protect your flyers.

- When you are walking, always hold a leash in your hand to give people a headsup that you're looking for a dog. Now is NOT the time to be shy. Talk to every single person you see. You can reduce the flyers to 1/4 or 1/8 size and hand them out as you walk.

The Long Haul

If your dog is lost for multiple days, it's time to bring out the big guns. You'll need to get eyes on them—either through flyers, a tracker, or a robocall—and then set up a live trap. Many local Animal Control departments and Humane Societies have these available to borrow. Get one large enough to comfortable hold your dog when it's closed.

Once you have identified a location that the dog is returning to at least once a day, set the live trap so that it is covered except for the entrance. Bales of hay come in handy for this. Attach a sign or one of your flyers to the trap to let people know why it's there. We also strongly recommend using a bike chain to attach the trap to a tree or fence. Because people suck.

Keep in mind that live traps can be notoriously hard to set. Take your time and make sure it is set up properly before leaving it. You will need to check the trap at least every couple of hours whenever it is open. If you can't get back in 3-4 hours to check the trap, leave it closed so no animals can get into it. Be prepared for feral cats, raccoons, other dogs, etc. in your trap.

To "bait" the trap you can put a worn article of clothing or bedding from the person the dog is the most attached to. An undershirt or pillowcase usually work well. Then use an inexpensive camp stove to fry 1-2 lbs of bacon right in front of the trap. After each batch, throw the bacon into the trap and drip the grease in trails leading toward the trap. Move quickly and as soon as you're done, leave the area so that you are not visible from the area of the trap.

When you've found your dog, either encountering them running loose or finding them caught in the trap, the most important thing is to stay calm and be very careful. So many people have reached for a loose dog's collar and ended up pulling it off, setting the dog loose again. Don't be that person.

A Case Study

Reyna, a Galgo from Spain, was one of the most traumatized dogs that SHUG had ever had in foster care. She had a fear of men that she struggled to overcome. This is all a roundabout way of saying Reyna is possibly the worst dog in the world to get loose during a walk.

Monday

But that's exactly what happened one bitterly cold day in January. Reyna's regular foster mom was away on vacation and her petsitter lost her hold on the leash during a walk. Near a busy highway. It was pretty much our worst nightmare.

If you've been paying attention, you may have noticed that one of the strengths of the sighthound community is our network of truly awesome volunteers. When the call came in on Monday afternoon, everyone mobilized. Volunteers took to the streets putting up flyers, to the woods searching, to the phones making calls, and to social media. When you've lost a dog, Facebook is your friend.

Within hours we had the word out and that meant sightings! Reyna's first day out, we spoke to literally a dozen people who saw her. She crisscrossed between the two main roads in the area, making a well-defined circle...then nothing. No sightings after 3 p.m. We ended the day cold and scared, knowing that she was, too.

Not too cold, though. One of our lucky breaks in this search was that Reyna was wearing a very distinctive purple coat. It made taking sighting information much easier. It also made Reyna much safer. Not only was the fleece coat warm and water resistant--it kept our pretty little fawn Spanish Greyhound from looking like a deer.

Tuesday

After a quiet night, action picked up again bright and early the next morning. By 7 a.m. Reyna was again making her well-defined circle across two busy streets, giving us all ulcers and permanent hair loss. Again, dozens of people saw her. When the phone would ring, the first question we would ask was *when!?* She was covering just a couple of miles, but her unauthorized shortcuts were much faster than our cars could travel by road. By the time we'd get up and around through several lights and over to her new location we'd get a call that she was already back on the other side of the highway.

By the end of the day, it seemed that Reyna had finally settled into one area. A church that backed onto a large park. Here's the twist...the church's large wooded property had been set up as a haunted "park." Over several acres of woods, there were school buses full of life size skeletons and clowns, multiple sheds and shacks full of staged scenes of headless dolls and other dismem-bered body parts. It was unbelievably creepy.

Our second lucky break in this search, was that it snowed that first night. Not enough to endanger Reyna, but enough to show footprints. Outside a little red barn full of hay in the middle of the haunted park, we found footprints--and a long straight line next to them in the snow, which looked like the trail of Reyna's leash. Inside the barn, a Reyna-sized indentation in the hay convinced us this is where she had spent the night.

The little red barn in the middle of the creepy woods became the center of our search and Reyna was seen there multiple times throughout Tuesday and late into the evening. Reyna's former foster mom left her tank top (fragrant after a day of traipsing through the woods) and something even more important—a live trap.

Wednesday

Nothing. Absolutely nothing. There were no sightings all day Wednesday. Volunteers checked the trap every couple of hours. We fielded texts and calls through the night but they were of sightings from the previous day. By noon, panic had set in. We had another trap donated by the local SPCA but our concern was that Reyna had been chased out of the area by the flurry of activity the previous day. Or worse. She could be caught by her leash somewhere deep in the woods. Volunteers scoured the area for any sign of her.

We had to stop and rethink our strategy. We made the decision to pull everyone out of the woods. We asked all volunteers to stay away from the area and refocus on putting up flyers the neighboring communities. That meant we would have to close the traps. It was just too cold to risk her getting caught in one if we weren't going to be checking them. And if we were checking them, we thought she wouldn't come back to the area. It was a classic Catch-22 scenario.

What made the situation slightly more bearable was the addition of cameras. Volunteers set up cameras near the little red barn and we all backed quietly out of the woods.

On other fronts, the search continued. Volunteers put up a new, more colorful version of the flyer, and we spammed thousands of people with a robocall. Within hours we had seven calls from people who had seen Reyna...the day before.

It was a very long night.

Thursday

We woke with a new plan. If Reyna didn't come back to the little red barn that day, we would have figure out her new location. To that end we contacted a tracker with a scent dog who had a good reputation with other rescues. As we were planning for the tracker and trying to find a good "scent" item of Reyna's, volunteers headed back to pull the memory cards from the cameras.

And ran right into Reyna at the little red barn!

The hunt was on again! Although Reyna ran away from them, they had her on film! Reyna had arrived back at the little red barn about an hour after we had vacated the woods the day before!! The time stamped pictures showed Reyna just hanging out, wandering around the area, eating the food we'd left, investigating the closed traps, and basically having a lovely vacation at the expense of our peace of mind.

Behold, the Power of Bacon

This was when we decided to bring out the big guns. We bought a camp stove and 3lbs of bacon. Just before noon, we set up the camp stove in the clearing in front of the little red barn and commenced **Operation: Bacon to the Rescue.** The cooked bacon went into the two traps, the grease was poured in a trail in front of them, and the smell went . . . EVERYWHERE. Around noon the trap was laid and the team retreated to the church parking lot.

An hour later, we checked the trap to find Reyna waiting patiently to be let out. She was wagging her tail and looking not at all sad to have been caught. Of course, she was also full of bacon.

Safe and Warm

The next two days were spent taking down all of the flyers, returning the borrowed traps, and updating every post on every page with the good news. Shockingly, Reyna was in excellent shape. Her pretty purple coat wasn't even dirty! She was a little dehydrated and did receive subcutaneous fluids, but she emerged from the haunted woods unscathed. I'm not sure the rest of us could say the same. That week definitely left a mark--but there were some great lessons learned. The most important lesson being that when sighthound people band together, they can move mountains.

LOST
GREYHOUND

DO NOT CHASE!

The Slip Knot

Yes, we are very paranoid about lost dogs. One of the best ways to prevent lost dogs, is by using a slip knot hold whenever your dog is not inside a fenced area. Simply put, the slip knot is your extra insurance. In order to make an effective slip knot, we recommend a simple 6ft nylon leash with a "loop" handle at the end. We do not recommend leashed with padded handles or grips.

The slip knot is made with the end of the leash over the hand on the opposite side from your dog. For example, if you are walking your dog on your right side, you will slip knot the loop of the leash over your left hand. You will still walk your dog with your right hand, but the "tail" of the leash will rest across your body and end at your left hand. This is your "emergency backup system".

Please note, the purpose of using a slip knot hold with your dog is to keep you and your dog together. In practice, this means that if your dog takes off and doesn't stop, you are going to be dragging on the ground after them. It is not necessary for your dog to outweigh you for this to happen. Greyhounds have been clocked at speeds of 45mph...and they can reach that speed in three strides. The longer your leash, the faster your dog will be going by the time they hit the end of it.

Your Step by Step Guide to the Slip Knot

These instructions assume you are walking your dog on your left side and slip knotting your right hand.

1. Holding the leash in your left hand, place your right hand through the loop of the leash.

2. Use your right hand to grab the leash just under the loop.

3. Drop the leash with your left hand, and use that hand to grab the loop resting over your right wrist.

4. Pull the loop over your right hand and about a foot down the length of the leash.

5. You should now be able to see the new loop that you've made. Since you're already holding onto it with your right hand, just "follow your fingers" through the new loop.

6. Grab the end of the leash and pull to tighten. You may also want to fuss with it for a moment to get everything nice and flat.

7. You now have a slip knot! Go walk your dog!

Separation Anxiety

Any dog can experience separation anxiety, but it is more common in dogs that have experienced loss or dramatic life changes—such as being abandoned, neglected, or abused. Just spending time in a kennel environment can be stressful for most sighthounds. Although racing Greyhounds are used to kennel environments before retirement, we have found that once these dogs have been in a home, going back to a kennel can be extraordinarily stressful for them.

In addition to barking and whining, signs of separation anxiety may include pooping and peeing inside, pacing, chewing or digging. It isn't always obvious whether these "bad behaviors" are caused by separation anxiety or a lack of training. One clear indicator is timing. If your dog only barks when you're gone or if they only have accidents when you leave them alone, that can be a sign that what you're dealing with is anxiety.

Please don't punish your dog for his anxious behavior, no matter how bad it is. They are acting out of anxiety and fear. Yelling will only make the situation worse. Compounding the problem is your dog's inability to connect your anger with a specific action that they took in the past. They don't know why you're angry or upset at them, and that's just going to increase their anxiety.

Reconditioning to Reduce Anxiety

You may never know the exact cause of your dog's separation anxiety. There may not have been one specific trigger. Sometimes many small experiences can add up to a big problem. But whatever the origin of their anxiety, it has conditioned them to expect **Big Bad Things** to happen when you are gone. In order to decrease—and hopefully over the long term—eliminate their anxious behaviors, you're going to have to change that conditioning.

There are several different strategies you can use to recondition your dog's reaction to separation. The main types are distraction, positive association, and chemical intervention. Using these three methods in combination can be highly effective.

For many dogs, a simple **distraction** from your absence can be enough to break the anxiety cycle. This strategy has two components. The first one is altering your patterns when you're getting ready to leave. As we know from human psychology, anticipation of pain can be worse than the actual pain itself. The moment you begin getting ready to leave the house, your dog starts getting anxious about the coming separation. If you can break that cycle, you can greatly reduce their initial anxiety.

The first step to break the **cycle of anticipation** is to identify the indicators of impending departure that your dog is picking up on. They can be things like picking up your keys, putting on your shoes, closing your laptop, etc. One adopter realized every time they got ready to leave, they sighed. Their dog started barking and running around the moment they sighed. Your dog may have similar triggers for meal times.

44

Once you've identified the triggers, try to eliminate them by either avoiding the behavior or by doing it more often when you're not leaving. For example, put your shoes on and walk around the house, or set them outside the door and put them on after you walk out. Pick up your keys and sit back down. You can also prepare to leave and then return immediately, or in five minutes. Do these things randomly throughout the day until your dog no longer responds to them. If you live with a partner, try using **code words** for common activities that might be triggers, as many of us have to do with W-A-L-K.

The second step is to implement distraction strategies that last after you've already left. These generally fall into two categories: **auditory** distractions and **chewable** distractions. When it comes to auditory distractions, there are several vendors who produce sounds specifically for dogs, but a light-hearted radio station can work just as well. Any kind of crafty or home improvement-based television channel can also be effective. It's very important to not tune into a station that includes programming that might have people yelling, crying (except tears of joy!) or otherwise in distress. That disqualifies most nature programs and day-time talk shows.

Chewable distractions include toys, bones, and treats. If your dog doesn't usually need to go out after breakfast, you can try giving them their meal and slipping out the door. A popular combination of a toy and a treat is to fill a hard rubber kong with peanut butter. Kongs come in multiple versions for all sizes of dogs and they can even be frozen to increase the longevity of the peanut butter (or cheese, dog-safe frozen dessert, etc.).

In addition to distracting your dog, chewable distractions can also provide **positive reinforcement**. Anything that your dog enjoys can become a positive reinforcement. In addition to treats, activities like walks and other exercise, objects—especially those that smell like you—and cuddly toys and beds can all be positive reinforcers. They're especially effective if they are exclusive to separation periods. For example, playing ball becomes a positive reinforcement if your pooch only gets to play on days that you have to go into the office.

The danger with making the association of separation with a positive reinforcer is that sometimes the anxiety is stronger than the positive feedback. In the example above, the owner could try to associate playing ball with them leaving the house...and soon the dog no longer enjoys playing ball. As soon as they see the ball they head for the hills. Now playing ball is a trigger.

In addition to activities, places can also become triggers for your dog's anxiety. If you place your dog in their **crate** every time you leave the house, the crate itself my cause the behaviors associated with separation anxiety, such as barking and accidents. It's good to have multiple methods to restrict your dog's movements while you're away. A metal x-pen or a baby-gated (and puppy-proofed) room are two good options. There are also different styles of crates and some dogs respond better to some than to others.

The third strategy for dealing with separation anxiety is **chemical intervention**. These come in three main forms. The first is the natural release of chemicals that your dog can get from **exercise**. Tiring them out before you have to leave them can decrease their anxiety and the physical symptoms of it. In addition, regular training in basic obedience can help your dog be generally more calm and confident.

The second type of chemical intervention is the plethora of **homeopathic** treatments, room air dispensers, collars, and other herbal remedies such as CBD that can help your dog remain calm and control their anxiety. Similarly, **prescription** medications can give your dog the ability to work through their fears. By keeping them from panicking and acting on their anxiety, it gives the dog a chance to realize that their fears are unfounded. It's important to discuss both over-the-counter and prescription drugs thoroughly with your vet before giving them to your dog. In many cases these treatments require weeks or even months to become effective and you must commit to a full course.

The Nuclear Option

For many dogs, the source of their separation anxiety is simply that they don't want to be alone. They're not worried about you or missing your particular company. They just feel sad and bored when they're alone. For those dogs, you may implement these strategies and eliminate the negative behavior associated with their anxiety, but your dog may be deeply unhappy. For those dogs, the best solution is to get them a canine (or even feline!) **companion** that stays in the house with them when you're gone.

Crate Training

Crates are a controversial topic among dog owners. Some people love them and some people hate them. At Sighthound Underground, we love them and think that they are a crucial part of any dog's training and safety. It is very likely that there will be times in your dog's life when it will be necessary for them to be crated.

Whether it is at the vet's office, during a long distance move, or during an emergency at an evacuation shelter, there are going to be times when the safest place for your dog will be in a crate. Even something like a burst pipe or large home improvement project could necessitate crate time for your dog while strange people walk in and out of your house. We have heard so many stories of dogs getting lost or hurt because a workman or a guest in the house opened a door or gave the dog an inappropriate treat. All of these dangers can be avoided if your dog has a crate and are comfortable using it.

Crate training is also a huge help in house training, curbing the destructive behavior of puppies and new dogs, managing food intake, and avoiding food aggression in multiple dog households. When introducing a new pet to any household, we strongly recommend crating or using another method to restrict their access during the adjustment period.

Once you've decided to crate train your dog, there are many different styles of crates to choose from. We recommend a simple, heavy duty, wire crate. These fold down flat for easy transport and storage, are easy to keep clean, and can easily be reinforced with zip ties. Once your dog is comfortable with their crate, many adopters find the "furniture" style crates to be a more attractive option in your home. Made of (fake) wicker or wood, or a combination of the two, these crates generally look like end tables and blend seamlessly into any decor. Hard plastic airline crates can be an option for some dogs as well. They can be awkward to move around, but they are excellent and containing messes. Many adopters have also tried the canvas collapsable travel style crates. Unless your dog is fairly bomb-proof, they're generally not going to be a good option.

Once you have your crate, the next decision is where to place it. Ideally, crates belong in human living spaces—either the living room/family room or the bedroom. Please don't put crates in bathrooms, garages, or other places where the dog will feel cut off from the main family interactions. This is again where the furniture style crates are nice, since they blend so well into living spaces.

There are four main circumstances under which you'll need to crate your dog on an average day: for meals, for bedtime, for when you're out of the house, and for when you are in the home but not able to watch them (for example, preparing dinner). The way you'll interact with the crate is different in each of these situations.

We highly recommend feeding your dog in the crate. Every meal and most treats should be given while they're in the crate when crate training. You can start by placing the food in the crate and walking away. We do try to avoid physically forcing the dog to go into the crate if possible. You may need to leave the room, but a high value treat should be enough to tempt them inside. In a multiple dog household, feeding in the crate makes it easy to see how much each dog is eating and avoids any fall out from food aggression.

Bedtime should progress similarly. A high value treat thrown in the back of the crate should tempt the dog to go in. If needed, you can guide them in with one hand on their collar and the other on their back end. Close the door, turn out the light, and go to bed. If your dog has gone to the bathroom prior to going to bed, ignore crying or whining. Be strong.

When you're leaving the house, a high value treat accompanied by a peanut butter-filled kong is your secret weapon. For longer absences, put the kong in the freezer the night before. It's important to not make a big deal out of leaving. Make sure there's a towel or fleece blanket in the crate, toss in the kong, and step away if necessary. When the dog has gone into the crate, close the door behind them and walk out the door. Do not say goodbye. Do not assure them repeatedly that mommy will hurry back. Pick up your keys and walk out the door. If you need to cry, do it in the car.

The forth scenario is the most complicated. When you need to crate your dog but you're not actually leaving the house, their objections can be vocal. And loud. This is definitely something to practice before that birthday party or special event when your house is full of strangers. The good news is that you'll use the same strategies as above, so every mealtime or departure is an opportunity to practice. If dinner is at 7pm, then crate your dog at 6:30pm. Leave them in there for five minutes, then just calmly open the door and walk away. Same thing with the kong. On

Saturday morning, complete your morning routine as if you're going to work. Throw the kong in the crate and shut the door. Then go and sit on the couch and read a book for an hour.

The last important tip for crate training your dog is to "be cool" when you let your dog out of the crate. Whether they were in the crate for a meal, or while you were having your own dinner, or while you went out to a movie, when you're ready to release them, don't make a big deal about it. Just open the door and walk away. If it's been a while and you need to take them out, try to do so with as little fanfare as possible. They aren't being released from a five year prison sentence. Don't throw a party!

A Reliable Recall

To veer into the financial world for a metaphor, a reliable recall isn't a CD—it's a holiday savings account. The kind of savings accounts people don't seem to have anymore, where you put in $5 a week and then get back a little nest egg just in time for Christmas. You have to "invest" in your recall on a regular basis. The longer you let it grow between "withdraws" the more bang you'll get for your buck when it's time to cash in.

The unfortunate reality is that we all need to make an investment in a reliable recall. No matter how careful you are, sometimes things happen outside of our control. You need a backup plan. We know you know the dangers of trust (which we'll talk about in a later chapter) and what to do in the minutes and hours (and—hopefully not—days) after your dog gets loose. But here's something that may pay off in those first seconds...and save you a lot of heartache.

So here are some tips to building a Really Reliable Recall. Keep in mind, just like your "water-resistant" watch, there is no such thing as a perfect recall. But following these steps will build a strong recall that may one day save your dog's life.

RULE #1: Set your dog up for success.

The most important rule of building a recall is to only practice it when you know it's going to work. How do you do that? Well, start out by using a long leash—or several leads clipped together. Set your dog up for success. Only give them a second to respond and start reeling them in like a fish. You need to start building the association in their minds that when you call, they come. No matter what.

Make sure you have a really great treat and that THEY KNOW IT! And make sure that you are the most interesting thing in their environment. Don't practice your recall in the backyard while your neighbor's intact poodle body slams the adjoining fence. That is definitely an advanced maneuver and you'd better be very sure of your dog before attempting it. You're much better off practicing in your living room, which is much less likely to be invaded by squirrels.

RULE #2: Do NOT use your dog's name.

Your recall is a very specific word or phrase that means "get your butt over here right now." Your dog's name means "look at me, I'm about to tell you something." This is a really important distinction for two reasons. Number one, your dog's name will never be a strong recall because you use it too much. You call their name dozens of times over the course of the day. Every time you call their name, you're making a "withdraw" from your Really Reliable Recall Savings Account. The second reason is that in an emergency, your dog may be quite far away from you when you spot him. If he's on the other side of a busy street you'll need to get his attention but you may not want him to automatically run to you.

So, if you aren't using their name, what are some examples of a recall cue? Well, every dog is different—and so is every owner. It has to be something that works for both of you. Generally, a recall should sound positive. For one of my Greyhounds, our recall was "Hey, Big Boy!" It was a phrase I never used in conversation and wasn't his actual nickname, but it really worked for us.

RULE #3: Invest in your recall!

Once you've figured out what your recall will be, it's time to start building in the "really reliable" part of it. You do that by practicing. A lot. This isn't a one-time effort. You may put a lot into your recall over the first week or so. Maybe you're having a staycation this year and for a week you're going to practice your recall three times a day. That's awesome! But you can't then forget about it until you need it. Maybe once a week, plan ahead and set yourself up for success. Do you have bacon and eggs on Saturday mornings? Save a piece of bacon for your dog. If you're still unsure of him, let him know you have the bacon before you call him. If you're pretty confident, let it be a pleasant
surprise.

Our last piece of advice is to remember to shake things up. Don't let yourself fall into a rut with your recall practice. When your dog is 100 percent reliable in the house, move the party outside. When he's got the backyard nailed, take your extra long lead to the local dog park early enough in the morning that you won't encounter anyone else. Or ask to borrow a friend's yard. Keep in mind that using the long lead with other off-lead dogs around is just asking for a dislocated shoulder.

We also don't recommend bringing bacon into an occupied dog park. Ever.

Good luck and have fun practicing your recalls! It will be the best investment we hope that you'll never have to cash in.

Basket Muzzles are Awesome

Racing Greyhounds wear plastic basket muzzles in the turn out pen and on the track. They keep the racers, which have very thin skin, safe as they play and run since many greyhounds have a tendency to nip in the excitement of the chase.

Those who adopt retired racers are generally encouraged to use muzzles, at least initially, and most find—often to their surprise—that the dogs really don't mind. These dogs have been wearing muzzles whenever they get to play or run so to them muzzles are a sign of good times.

To someone who has never owned a retired racing Greyhound, though, a muzzle may invoke images of aggression and restraint. And while there are muzzles for aggressive dogs, basket muzzles are very different. For one thing, it doesn't restrict their mouth from opening and closing, and they can eat and drink while wearing a basket muzzle. (NOTE: even a basket muzzle might inhibit a dog's ability to pant so always monitor your dog when it's warm.)

As you may have already figured out, the Sighthound Underground is a big fan of basket muzzles—and not just for Greyhounds. We think they are a "must have" in every sighthound home. Those first couple of days when you're leaving your new dog loose in your home, a basket muzzle ensures you still have a completely intact couch—even if some idiot carpet salesman knocks on your door while you're at work. When transporting dogs too big to be crated, $10 muzzles can prevent $500 vet bills when an abrupt traffic stop causes a pileup in the back seat. A muzzle is a handy tool when making introductions between new dogs or a new dog and a cat. A muzzle can also—with the addition of the aptly named "stool guard"—prevent the dreaded poop-scented kisses after a romp in the backyard.

Borzoi, Galgos, Salukis, and Afghan Hounds may not have the history with basket muzzles that Greyhounds do, but we've seen those breeds easily sporting the dashing accessory. While we occasionally have one who expresses his or her displeasure by smacking your backside with the muzzle, for the most part non-racers are as nonchalant about their headgear as retired racers.

Once you've decided to give it a try, how do you put on a muzzle? First, have it right-side up. There will be a smooth, rounded or even padded section that goes on the top. Once you have the muzzle in the right position, pull the ear strap forward toward the basket and slip the basket over your dog's nose. Then you can bring the strap over their forehead and behind their ears. The strap has a buckle to adjust the size if it's too tight or too loose.

In a well-fitting muzzle, the tip of the dog's nose doesn't quite touch the inside end of the muzzle and the strap is easy to pull behind their ears but not so loose as to pop off with the swipe of a paw. (You can also buy a special strap for your muzzle that connects the ear strap to your dog's collar, if necessary.) If your dog has particularly sensitive skin, you can add a piece of moleskin or fleece against the inside of the nose piece at the top of the basket to provide some padding.

Muzzles can also be quite the fashion accessory! They come in a variety of colors and while most of us are content to simply write our dog's name across the top with a sharpie, there are some (you know who you are!) who go all out with the stick-on gems and glitter.

It helps that muzzles are fairly inexpensive (usually under $10) and can be ordered online at several different retailers. Keep in mind that most greyhounds wear a medium (girls or small boys) or large (big boys); borzoi may need extra large for those awesome extra long needle noses.

The Dog Park Problem

The Sighthound Underground is not a big fan of dog parks. In fact, we're officially against taking your sighthound to a public dog park.

All too often we've seen unfamiliar dogs get aggressive or small dogs get frisky and try to "run with the big dogs." Either way, someone gets hurt. And while it's usually the dog owner who is to blame when things go awry, it's almost always the dog that pays the price.

SHUG does endorse private dog parks—with screening policies—and "play dates" with familiar dogs. We also encourage sighthound owners to consider using basket muzzles whenever dogs will be running together. They won't hurt your dog and may save you—and your fellow dog owners—the pain and expense of an injury.

Whether at a dog park or on a play date in your own living room, always pay attention when dogs play and take note of these signs. When dogs display one or more of these behaviors it can mean that it's time for a break:

- One of the dogs is trying to move away or hide from the other. This can take the form of trying to squeeze into a tight space or trying to climb onto a human.

- One of the dogs is crying or whimpering. While many dogs do vocalize during play, pay attention to the sounds and don't just "tune it out". If the tenor changes, it may be time to intervene.

- The energy levels between one or both of the dogs becomes too high. When dogs become too excited, accidents can happen—especially when you're dealing with thing sighthound skin.

Making sure play stays fun for everyone is the dog owner's responsibility. If you're not sure, take your dog for a walk instead. That's always a good thing!

Better Living Through Chemistry

Fearful dogs need more than hugs. Sometimes, they need drugs. Most often, dogs who have anxiety can benefit from anti-anxiety medication to help them "over the hump". Just calming their anxiety a little bit can let them be brave enough to explore their environment. Once they've seen what's around the corner, everything can feel a lot less scary.

Below, we talk specifically about one of our toughest cases. Every dog is different, and if your dog is suffering from anxiety or fear-based aggression, we strongly recommend that you have a conversation with your veterinarian about medications that can improve their quality of life.

A Case Study

When the rescue community received the news that the CDC was banning dogs from over 100 countries in June of 2021, there was a mad scramble. The ban went into effect in 29 days and dogs must be vaccinated 30 days before entry to the US, so there wasn't enough time to prepare dogs who weren't already vetted. Groups focused on evacuating dogs from countries like Qatar who were "ready to fly" to make room for the dogs that would come in over the months that would follow. (At the time, the CDC was already warning that the ban would be in place for at least one year. As of now there's no sign of it being lifted anytime soon.)

Right before the deadline, the Sighthound Underground had one more spot on our last flight out of Qatar. One of our partners asked us to consider Aquila the Saluki, who they described as a "feral" dog. At the time, in the shock and desperation of the days following the announcement of the ban, we were eager to help wherever we could. Even in hindsight we would have said yes...but it's easy to see now that we didn't really know what we were getting into.

Sighthounds are unique in the dog world for their extraordinarily long history as companions to humans. Greyhounds make appearances in the Bible and Homer's *Odyssey*. For thousands of years they have been bred to work alongside their people. We see sighthounds that have been neglected and abused...but feral? That is much less common in the sighthound world.

When Aquila arrived, he was indeed a feral dog. He'd been caught in the Qatari desert, and he wanted to return there. He hated life in a home, wearing a collar and constrained by a leash or harness. He had zero trust in humans and constantly growled and/or ran from his foster mom. No matter what treats she tried, no matter what voice she used, he wanted nothing to do with her.

Another hallmark of sighthounds and a result of the specialized way they have been bred for millennia, is their lack of aggression toward humans. We rarely see sighthounds who bite.

Aquila bit.

In those first weeks he bit his foster mom every time she attempted to touch him or put a leash or harness on him. Never hard enough to break the skin, but he made his feelings known. Aquila was not aggressive—his nips were his reaction to his anxiety and his fear of humans—but they still hurt!

We started him on trazodone. Soon after another foster arrived in Aquila's foster home, a little Whippet from Hawaii named Giza. He bonded quickly with her...drawn to her confidence and playfulness. Within a couple of weeks we saw his anxiety and fear begin to fade. Aquila started to be more accepting of human contact and began sleeping near his foster mom and approaching her for attention. We still had a lot to work on, but it was a good start.

With his friend Giza leading the way, Aquila started to play and enjoy his life. He loved playing with toys, chasing, and wrestling on a dog bed. He began to approach his foster mom now without fear—and she could approach him without worrying about nipping.

Aquila's anxiety disappeared. He let his foster mom hug him, and put on his leash and harness without any fuss. He began to attend public events and—by his own choice—went out of the 'booth area' to meet strangers, and readily accepted their pets and ear rubs....truly enjoying all the attention. It was there that Aquila and Giza met the family that would adopt them. Together.

Aquila is still on trazodone, and may be for years. It is possible that he will need a maintenance dose for the rest of his life. Be he has worked hard to find his happy, and now he's in the right home to help him keep it.

Aquila may have started out as a feral dog, but today he is a wonderful, easy companion.

Your Dog is Fat

We've had this conversation so many times, with so many people. We struggle to find a diplomatic way to tell people that their dog has gained a little too much weight, but often it takes a more direct approach. Generally, the conversation starts out something like this...

Your dog is fat.

We know this comes as a terrible shock—and it doesn't mean your Greyhound or Saluki or Borzoi isn't beautiful and sweet and well-loved. It does, however, mean that your dog has a fifty percent greater chance of developing cancer. Yes, that's right, cancer. The big C. And if that doesn't scare you straight (or your dog skinny) your dog is also at risk for other health problems—ranging from severe joint pain to heart and kidney issues—that will profoundly impact their quality of life.

How does this happen?

Well, quite easily, unfortunately. This is especially true for new sighthound parents, who are used to having other breeds. You didn't make your sighthound fat because you didn't care—you made it fat because you cared too much. When you picked up your greyhound from the track or your galgo from the airport he was very, very thin. It broke your heart and you made it your mission to put weight on him. You've succeeded a bit too well.

The problem is your sighthound is not a lab. Take a look at the picture below.

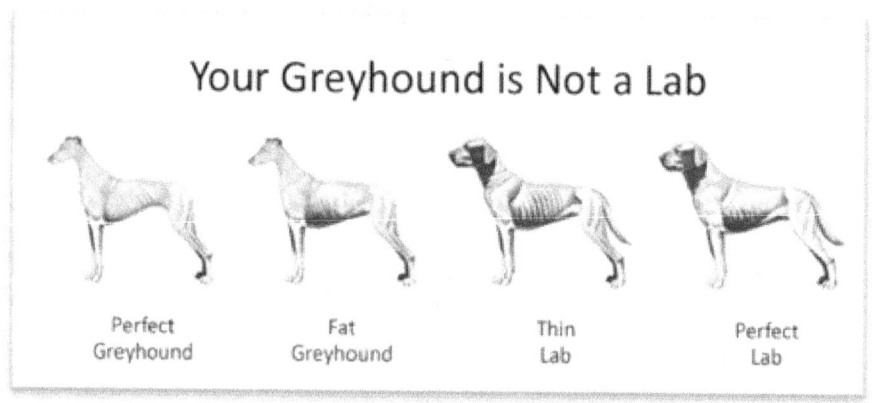

Your Greyhound is Not a Lab

| Perfect | Fat | Thin | Perfect |
| Greyhound | Greyhound | Lab | Lab |

A fat Greyhound looks just like a thin lab (with an unusually pointy noise and severe narcolepsy). If this was your first sighthound and you'd only ever seen "normal" dogs before, then the "fresh from the track or kennel" thinness was very alarming. It may have also been alarming to your friends and neighbors who, upon meeting your new dog, repeatedly admonished you to "feed that dog!"

Well, shame on you for giving in to peer pressure! If your sighthound has gained more than five pounds since he or she came to your home, you need to take a step back—literally, back away from the dog—and take a good look. How many ribs can you see? From across the room you should be able to see the first three. Can you see his hip pins? On some Sighthounds you can even see their vertebrae—gasp!--and that's totally okay. If you have a Borzoi or an Afghan, take a look the next time you're giving them a bath. How much dog--exactly--is there under all of that hair?

When you have come to grips with the emotional trauma of realizing that your sighthound is, in fact, fat . . . the time has come to un-fattify your dog. (Yes, we're sure that's a word.) Keep in mind that it is often a good idea to consult your veterinarian before any drastic diet changes. Just reducing the amount of kibble they receive every day may negatively affect their behavior. Switching to a lower calorie food, or a food with a different protein may make the adjustment easier on both of you.

"Trust, A Deadly Disease"

by Sharon Mathers

There is a deadly disease stalking your dog. A hideous, stealthy thing just waiting its chance to steal your beloved friend. It is not a new disease, or one for which there are no inoculations. The disease is called trust.

You knew before you ever took your Greyhound home that it could not be trusted. The people who provided you with this precious animal warned you, drummed it into your head. A newly rescued racer may steal off counters, destroy something expensive, chase cats, and must never be allowed off his lead!

When the big day finally arrived, heeding the sage advice, you escorted your dog to his new home, properly collared and tagged, the lead held tightly in your hand. At home the house was "doggie proofed." Everything of value was stored in the spare bedroom, garbage stowed on top of the refrigerator, cats separated, and a gate placed across the door to the living room. All windows and doors had been properly secured and signs placed in strategic points reminding all to "CLOSE THE DOOR".

Soon it becomes second nature to make sure the door closes a second after it was opened and that it really latched. "DON'T LET THE DOG OUT" is your second most verbalized expression. (The first is NO!) You worry and fuss constantly, terrified that your darling will get out and a disaster will surely follow. Your friends comment about who you love most, your family or the dog. You know that to relax your vigil for a moment might lose him to you forever.

And so the weeks and months pass, with your Greyhound becoming more civilized every day, and the seeds of trust are planted. It seems that each new day brings less mischief, less breakage. Almost before you know it your racer has turned into an elegant, dignified friend.

Now that he is a more reliable, sedate companion, you take him more places. No longer does he chew the steering wheel when left in the car. And darned if that cake wasn't still on the counter this morning. And, oh yes, wasn't that the cat he was sleeping with so cozily on your pillow last night? At this point you are beginning to become infected, the disease is spreading its roots deep into your mind.

And then one of your friends suggests obedience. You shake your head and remind her that your dog might run away if allowed off the lead, but you are reassured when she promises the events are held in a fenced area. And, wonder of wonders, he did not run away, but came every time you called him!

All winter long you go to weekly obedience classes. After a time you even let him run loose from the car to the house when you get home. Why not, he always runs straight to the door, dancing a frenzy of joy and waits to be let in. Remember, he comes every time he is called. You know he is the exception that proves the rule. (And sometimes, late at night, you even let him slip out the front door to go potty and then right back in.) At this point the disease has taken hold, waiting only for the right time and place to rear its ugly head.

Years pass—it is hard to remember why you ever worried so much when he was new. He would never think of running out the door left open while you bring in the packages from the car. It would be beneath his dignity to jump out the window of the car while you run into the convenience store. And when you take him for those wonderful long walks at dawn, it only takes one whistle to send him racing back to you in a burst of speed when the walk comes too close to the highway. (He still gets into the garbage, but nobody is perfect.)

This is the time the disease has waited for so patiently. Sometimes it only has to wait a year or two, but often it takes much longer.

He spies the neighbor dog across the street, and suddenly forgets everything he ever knew about not slipping outdoors, jumping out windows, or coming when called due to traffic. Perhaps it was only a paper fluttering in the breeze, or even just the sheer joy of running—

Stopped in an instant. Stilled forever—your heart is broken at the sight of his still beautiful body. The disease is trust. The final outcome, hit by a car.

Every morning my dog Shah bounced around off his lead exploring. Every morning for seven years he came back when he was called. He was perfectly obedient, perfectly trustworthy. He died fourteen hours after being hit by a car. Please do not risk your friend and your heart. Save the trust for things that do not matter.

I would like to offer two additional accounts about the dangers of an unfenced area.

This first account is really a basic tragic accident, due to an improperly fitting collar. The owners actually had the dog on a lead, but unfortunately were using only a flat buckle collar on the dog. The dog became frightened at something, and just backed out of her collar. She took off away from them at top speed. Before they could manage to even get close to catching up to her, she had run out onto a road, and was instantly killed by a car. This is one of the reasons we advise using a halter[1] while walking your Greyhound in an unfenced area.

The second account involves too much trust and a lack of common sense. The owners lived somewhat out in the country. Their home was surrounded by woods and they were well off any major roadway. They had their new Greyhound about three weeks, when I got the phone call that I hate the most, "Our Greyhound is lost!" I knew these owners did not have a fenced yard, but they had sworn they would keep the dog on a lead when taken outdoors. Upon further questioning, I discovered that they quit using the lead after about the first week. The weather had gotten cold, and so early in the mornings they would simply turn her out the back door, wait for her to "do her business," then call her back in. "She ALWAYS came when she was called," the woman lamented to me. They felt it was safe enough to allow her off the lead for just short bits of time, as they didn't live near a high traffic road, and she had never ventured into the woods before. Unfortunately, the little Greyhound DID bound off into the woods this particular morning. Perhaps she heard a squirrel rustling in some nearby leaves, or smelled a rabbit, but whatever the reason, she had taken off into the woods, and they could not find her. Our hopes of finding her safe and sound faded a little more with each passing day, and no sign of the pretty little female Greyhound.

After several weeks, our worst fears were confirmed. We got a call from a very nice man, who had been walking through the woods with his son when they discovered the still, cold body of a small, dead Greyhound. He got our number off her collar ID tag. She was found many, many miles from her home.

Why did she run off this time when she had been so reliable before? Why didn't she come racing back as she always had when her family called for her? Who knows? What we do know is that ultimately dogs will be dogs. No matter how much or how long you train and teach your dog, there may come a point where their instincts will win over learned behavior. Please don't be fooled into a false sense of security with your Greyhound. Take the time, make that little extra effort, to ensure your Greyhound will be safe.

Remember, they are depending on you.

Reprinted with the author's permission.

---

1. NOTE: We recommend using martingale collars for all sighthounds. If you are going to use a halter, we urge you to only use three ring style harnesses. This type has a loop in front of the front legs, behind the front legs, and around the dog's waist or "tuck". We also recommend using a small safety strap to attach the harness to a martingale collar and to attach the leash to the martingale.

Published April 1987 *New England Obedience News*

Published 1988 in *Canine Concepts and Community Animal Control Magazine*

Courtesy of *Canine Concepts and Community Animal Control magazine.*

Compliments of: *New Hampshire Doberman Rescue League, Inc.*

About the Author

Ms. Michael Owens is a single mother, artist, author, and certified Crazy Dog Lady. She lives with her daughter and an unreasonable number of dogs in an old yellow farmhouse by the sea.

After volunteering with multiple rescues for over a decade, Michael founded the Sighthound Underground in 2012. She has served as a regional coordinator for the Italian Greyhound Club of America, a foster coordinator for Greyt Expectations Greyhound Rescue, and fostered for the National Borzoi Rescue Fund.

She has fostered Greyhounds, Galgos, Borzoi, Salukis, Afghan Hounds, Whippets, Italian Greyhounds, Azawakhs, Scottish Deerhounds, Irish Wolfhounds, Ibizan Hounds, Great Danes, Great Pyrenees, Newfoundlands, Komondors, Standard Poodles, Terriers, Chihuahuas, and the occasional cat.

The Sighthound Underground is a 501(c)3 public charity. You can find more information at http://sighthoundunderground.com. Questions about this book or the Sighthound Underground can be directed to info@sighthoundunderground.com.

www.ingramcontent.com/pod-product-compliance
Lightning Source LLC
Chambersburg PA
CBHW051008140626
46546CB00016B/1350

* 9 7 8 1 9 5 8 5 5 9 0 5 5 *